PROTECTING YOUR BUSINESS
FROM
INSIDER THREATS
IN SEVEN EFFECTIVE STEPS

HOW TO IDENTIFY, ADDRESS AND SHAPE THE HUMAN ELEMENT OF THE THREAT
WITHIN YOUR BUSINESS IN SEVEN SUCCESSFUL PRACTICES

BOAZ FISCHER

FIRST EDITION 2017
Copyright © 2017 by CommsNet Group

All rights reserved. No part of this publication may be reproduced, stored in retrieval system or transmitted in any form or by any means, electronic, mechanical, photocopying, recording or otherwise without prior written permission from the author.

Every reasonable effort has been made to contact a copyright holders of material reproduced in this book. If you have any inadvertently been overlooked, the publishers would be glad to hear from you and make good in future editions any errors or omissions brought to their attention.

National Library of Australia
Cataloguing-in-Publication entry:

Boaz Fischer
Protecting Your Business from Insider Threats In Seven Effective Steps
1st ed.

ISBN 978-0-9925809-1-9

9 780992 580919 >

Dedication

*I'm dedicating this book to all those businesses,
organisations and other entities,
who have invested much time and effort
in protecting their businesses assets.*

*My intention is to inspire you, to help you, and to push you
into adopting best practices for protecting your assets
so that your business flourishes
and the people that you touch are transformed.*

*There is no such thing as a "Silver Bullet" when it comes to security.
And there is no such thing as a "Perfect Harmonious Society".
People are your biggest asset and yet they are your biggest risk.*

*At the end of the day, the goals are simple:
Safety and Security.*

ACKNOWLEDGMENT

I am grateful to a number of individuals who have helped me make this book a reality.

At the top of the list is Scott Deacon who grabbed the book with zeal and wrote lots of notes from cover to cover. Thank you my friend.

Secondly, I would like to thank Sean Ofir from SABASAI who has offered lots of positive and constructive feedback. Great to have a colleague in the same field of interest.

I have also received valuable reviews, feedback and critiques along the way from James Fitzell, Andrew Hammond, Nigel Hedges, Michael O'Flaherty, Paul Steen and Trevor Plant. Thank you all.

I would also like to thank Sarah Van Heertum from 3 Moutons Studio for her wonderful graphics and outlays of the book.

I would like to thank Margaret Walker from DiverseDocumenteur for her wonderful and helpful book editing.

I would like to thank the Insider Threat Division of CERT (Software Engineering Institute | Carnegie Mellon University) for providing a great resource and information about Insider Threats.

Draft of the book... Oh, so many drafts, you have no idea how difficult it is to write a short, simple book, which is scrutinised and found wanting by many of my friends and colleagues. I am grateful to them all.

Finally, thanks to my colleagues back at work – Oren Fischer, Nunzio Grassia, Maurice Consen, Melissa Maher, and Jacinta Small.

Last but not least, I would like to thank my wife Alexandra, and my little boy, Ilan for their patience and love.

FOREWORD

Damage and the risk of damage from trusted insiders is certainly not a new phenomenon. One need only consider some of our earliest recorded stories, be they religious or secular works, to see memorable examples of both malicious and unintentional insider threats that have caused damage and sorrow. While most of those stories have focused on events affecting only an individual there has also always been the threat from individuals that can affect an entire organization (public and private). I would bet that Julius Caesar wished he had read this book before trusting his fate and that of the organization to Brutus.

Unfortunately, I too am not new to malicious and unintentional insider threats. After spending more than 25 years in the U.S. Intelligence Community as a Counterintelligence Special Agent; I have accumulated far more than my share of these stories. Couple that experience with my more than 30 years of concurrent work in cybersecurity and you might begin to imagine how I ended up working at Carnegie Mellon University's 'CERT Insider Threat Center' (a program within the university's Software Engineering Institute).

Mr. Fischer has spent a lot of time reviewing much of the peer-reviewed empirical research, well documented case studies, and collected best practices for preventing, detecting, and responding to threats from trusted insiders. This is an important consideration when reading any 'How-To' book.

I will tell you from personal experience that it is all too easy to fall into a mindset wherein our own observations, if encountered enough times, become considered by us as solid fact. However, the conclusions from these anecdotal observations are notably different from actual scientific fact. Think of that old cautionary analogy of, "well everyone that did that thing had a nose, so everyone who has a nose must…" I thought because of my previous experience I knew everything there was to know about insider threat. But once I was able to study the peer-reviewed research and participate in the scientific investigation of insider threats I realized I had some errant conclusions about malicious and unintentional insiders.

As you begin to read this book, I would like to share this concept for you to consider. There is a theory that I have been continually refining for over three decades. The hypothesis is this: It takes only three principles working in concert, to protect yourself, your family, or your organization from insider threats. Think of it like a three-legged stool. If one of the legs is missing, the stool will most likely not support you. Or better yet, a pie with only three slices. If one of the slices is cut a bit smaller, one or both of the other slices needs to be larger in order for it to still be considered a complete pie.

The first leg (or slice): You must accurately judge trust. This may sound simple, but it really is not. We conduct background checks on potential employees before we hire them and decide if we have trust in them. However, research has shown that insider threat fraud often does not start until after an employee has worked for the company for at least five years. Do you have processes in place to continually re-evaluate that initial judgement of trust?

The second leg (or slice): You must right-size permissions. People should be able to accomplish what you expect them to, but not be able to freely perform tasks outside of what you intend. Again, this sounds easy. In the cyber realm we have a lot of tools that can enforce role-based permissions. And in the physical world, we issue keys for locks, badges for card readers, and pin numbers at access points. But how do you prevent someone with exceptional knowledge, skills, or access, from exceeding these controls. For example, how do you prevent a computer system administrator from changing their own permissions to allow them greater access to your systems? Or prevent the key custodian from creating another master key for themselves?

And the third leg (or slice): You must conduct effective monitoring. An adage attributed to retired U.S. Navy Admiral Hyman G. Rickover states "You don't get what you expect, only what you inspect." Having a policy, guidance, or procedures does not mean that is how things actually get done. There must be a way of monitoring that confirms this.

Here are two examples of how these three principles work together. One example is from the cyber realm, and one is from the world of bricks and mortar.

Cyber Example: The organization's has a policy that only USB devices (removable media) that are owned by the company can be attached to the company's network. A trusted insider attaches a USB device to the company network. Because there is effective monitoring in place, the device attachment is detected. The USB is inspected and is determined to belong to the company, so the device is allowed to mount as a drive and files can be transferred to and from the device. We know from this that the permissions are in-fact 'right sized' and that the judgement of trust in that employee has been revalidated. In a reverse example, a trusted insider attaches a USB device they brought in from home (or found in a parking lot, or got at a trade show/convention) and they attach the device to the company network. Because effective monitoring is in place, we know that the USB device does not belong to the company and therefore, the device is blocked from mounting as a drive and no files can be read or written to the device. So we have re-validated that the permissions are still 'right sized' but maybe our judgement of trust in the employee should be revisited. Perhaps it is time for this employee to receive some additional training on the company's 'acceptable use policy'?

Physical Example: You are leaving a store late at night. The parking lot is not well lit and there are not a lot of people around – maybe just a few people who might also be walking to their car. Or maybe, they are just waiting for you to unlock your car before they make their move? Because you are effectively monitoring the situation (fully aware of your surroundings) you ensure the car doors stay locked until you (and only you) can enter the vehicle. Once safely inside the car you lock the doors and continue to monitor if anyone is approaching as you put the car in gear and leave the parking lot. Because you did not have an accurate judgment of trust in the other people in the parking lot you needed to effectively monitoring your surroundings. And you unlocked and re-locked your doors in the best way to 'right-size' permissions.

My personal and professional research has exposed me to hundreds upon hundreds of scenarios and I have not yet encountered one where these three principles did not apply. I think Boaz' Seven Effective Principles not only have a good application for any type of organization, but they also reinforce the three principles that I laid out here.

I would be extremely interested in hearing your thoughts as you read through this book. Let me know whether my three principles have efficacy (or might be lacking) when considering Mr. Fischer's Seven Effective Steps.

Michael C. Theis
Special Agent in Charge (retired), CISSP
Assistant Director for Research and Senior Member of the Technical Staff
CERT Insider Threat Center
Software Engineering Institute (an FFRDC)
Carnegie Mellon University

TABLE OF CONTENTS

A NOTE TO _____ THE READER

"You mean that was an INSIDE Job?", the CEO asks.

That's the last sentence any executive wants to hear, especially when evidence confirms that the actions of someone within the organisation caused harm to the organisation.

"How did it happen?" That's a good question.

"Why didn't we find out sooner?" A difficult question to answer.

"How bad is it?" Don't know yet.

"Who else is involved?" Don't know.

"How long has this been going on?" Still looking into that.

Unfortunately, questions like this are becoming more of a standard situation upon discovering that someone has caused an insider breach.

"Insider Threat" has become an industry buzzword, stemming largely from the massive data breach that was perpetuated by former US National Security Advisor and contractor, Edward Snowdon.

Yet, a majority of insider threats are far less conspicuous. Less conspicuous threats won't make headlines and most are unintentional, but they may cause massive damage and potentially shut down the business.

While many organisations have recognised the "threat from within", little attention or effort is placed on appropriately protecting corporate assets.

Despite a massive investment in infrastructure and endpoint security, large organisations continue to fall victim to this type of threat each week. The arrest of National Security Agency contractor Thomas Martin III, charged with stealing highly classified material, is the latest example.

Why? At its core, we are dealing with people and not machines. We are dealing with the dynamics of people and their behaviour. We mistakenly think that all people have a uniform behaviour and as such, they conform to a uniform set of rules. Yet, this assumption is erroneous, and this thinking is one of the gravest errors management and executives can make. Every employee has a set of needs, values, unique beliefs, thoughts, and definitely unique motivations, and some of these variations may not be congruent with the organisation goals or culture.

Given the diversity of behaviour that is possible, it can be extremely difficult to discern the trustworthy from the untrustworthy.

Trust is confidence, and a lack of trust is suspicion. A survey conducted by British Sociologist David Halpern reveals that only 34% of Americans believe that other people can be trusted. In Latin America, the number is 23%, and in Africa, the figure is 18%.

Today's news headlines reveal the symptoms of the compelling truth. Low trust is everywhere. It permeates in our global society, our work, our relationships and our lives resulting in a costly downward spiral.

So, how do most organisations tackle the potential threat from within? They do this by building more borders, more controls, and more policies. Conventional thinking and strategies overemphasize firewall protection, intrusion protection, and endpoint protection. These forms of protection are often labelled the "Defence in Depth" strategy. However, I call it the "Egg Defence" Practice; the outside is hard and brittle, but inside its soft and gooey.

This is the question that you need to ask: Do the investments you have made in security solutions and controls thus far, empower greater user engagement? Do they engender greater trust, collaboration, creativity, and innovation within the team? If they do not, you are most likely promoting an environment of distrust.

Yes, we need to recognise that the insiders pose security risks due to their legitimate access to facilities, technology and information. They know where the most valuable data is located. They know how to get it, and, if they want to, they know how to get around the security controls. But trying to lock them in, hasn't worked well so far, and spending more on controls and hoping that the problem will disappear, simply does not work. Look no further than NSA.

WHY THIS BOOK?

I wrote this book because I see a massive need to address a serious problem that very few organisations are focusing on – and the lack of awareness about the threat from within is extremely worrisome.

Insider Threat is fast becoming one of the biggest threats in today's environment. Yet, the majority of budgets focus primarily on protecting against external threats.

The Verizon 2015 Data Breach Investigation Report indicates that 90% of all incidents stem from people, and a variety of circumstances (goofing up, getting infected, behaving badly, or just plain losing stuff).

Today's data breach news will not be any different next week or next month. Yes, we read about the consequences, but we do not realise that the root cause for a majority of the cases is self-inflicted.

Data breaches do not happen by themselves! There is always a cause and effect situation. The cause is, someone clicked on a link and got compromised. The effect is stolen data. Or, the cause is someone left a database of passwords on an unprotected system. The effect, due to very poor security practices, an attacker is allowed to steal all credentials and hack their way into the organisation's sensitive data.

The breach of Target is another example of severely poor security practices. In December 2013, the theft of over 40 million credit cards from nearly 2000 Target stores was accomplished by accessing data on point of sale (POS) systems.

The Office of Personal Management (OPM) breach was the result of a cascading series of cybersecurity blunders from the agency's senior leadership, down to the outdated technology used to secure the sensitive data. The massive data breach exposed background investigations and fingerprint data on millions of Americans.

The breach of Sony exposed careless security practices, which are not unusual. The result: Hackers not only erased data from Sony systems, but also stole and released to the public, pre-release movies, people's private information and sensitive documents.

So why This Book?

I have been writing on the subject of information security best practices for many years. I have written over 100 articles and 2 books. The common theme has always been about the "Human" element of security. Back in 1999, Bruce Schneier, a very well respected security expert, coined this phrase about security: *security is a combination of "people-processes-technology"*. Bruce went on to argue that because of the ever-increasing system complexity, we need less in the way of people and process, and more technology. I disagree!

So here is the problem.

You can have the best set of security technologies, but if they are poorly configured, then you have a big gaping hole.

You can have the best set of processes and policies, but if they are not followed, then again, your leave yourself wide open.

You can have the best of technologies and automation, including strong set of policies and controls, but if the person is motivated to commit a malicious act, they will and they can. Look no further than the acts of the latest NSA contractor Harold Martin, who is accused of stealing 50 terabytes worth of classified information dating back to 1996.

We really need to address the human element of security as part of the equation more than ever.

Protecting Your Business From Insider Threats In Seven Effective Steps is a book for any organisation that is serious about protecting their key assets. If you employ people, work with other companies, and/or allow 3rd party organisations to access your data, then you are agreeing, in principal, that you trust these people because they may place your organisation at risk.

Protecting Your Business From Insider Threats In Seven Effective Steps addresses seven potential signs that indicate you may already be compromised by an insider. My goal in this book is to show you how this type of breach can occur, and more importantly, what tasks and considerations you may take to mitigate such threats.

Consider this quote made by Robert S. Mueller, III, FBI Director:
"There are only two types of companies: Those that have been hacked and those that will be hacked."

Perhaps the statement should be:
"There are only two types of companies: Those that have been hacked and those that don't know they have been hacked."

"There is no security patch for stupidity, deliberate or not."

No matter how good or strong your technology defences are (firewalls, anti-virus software, intrusion detection systems) or how robust your internal controls and processes are, your people remain the weakest link. It is analogous to driving a car – there are road rules, line markings, and warning signs, and people still ignore or disregard them.

INTRODUCTION

What is the common denominator of organisations of all types? People, people make up organisations.

People work and contribute to the value, benefit, profit, advantage, and to the role of the organisation within the marketplace.

How resilient is your organisation, given that it is run by people?

How do you know which user may pose a threat to your organisation, either maliciously or unintentionally?

Every organisation wants to believe their employees are beyond reproach.

Every organisation wants to believe their employees are trustworthy.

Every organisation assumes their employees have the best intentions towards their organisation.

Let me debunk this theorem.

Right now, you have no mechanism or tool to control people's behaviour.

Behaviour is the result of the "frames", (the inner executive), that drive human actions. These frames govern an individuals' state of mind and emotions. They are the beliefs, perception, values, ideas, agendas, desires, thoughts, mission, identity, skills, motivation and destiny of a person.

When people go to work, they bring with them their own frames, which may contain some negative behaviour. It is important to note, that no organisation has the ability to control a persons' behaviour. Sure, they can threaten them; they can demean them; they can abuse them, they can try and control them, but ultimately, each person owns their own frame.

Without much thought, organisations readily trust their employees. But who are their employees, really?

A trusted insider is anyone that operates within the organisation who has an authorised identity. The key aspect of such a user is access to organisation assets and applications, including confidential data.

A trusted Insider can be any person who has access to the organisation assets including past employees, sub-contractors, partners, consultants, vendors, and friends.

How do you know if a person in your employ has "harmed" your organisation trust?

The Insider Threat Division within CERT defines of a malicious Insider is one who meets the criteria below. (CERT is Computer Emergency Response Team, in particular, this reference is to CERT Insider Threat Division at Carnegie Mellon University.)

Has or had authorised access to organisation assets; and

Has intentionally exceeded or intentionally used that access in a manner that negatively affects the "confidentiality, integrity, and availability" of the organisation assets.

An insider can pose a massive threat to your business because they have knowledge of, and access to, your systems and information. They can easily bypass physical and electronic security measures through legitimate means.

Insiders have knowledge of the location of valuable assets. They know how, when, and where to attack, and how to cover their tracks. Insiders can target an asset directly, and do not need to overcome the barriers external hackers face.

Most important, malicious Insiders have time on their side. They have a much larger window of opportunity to do greater harm, more quickly and much faster because access to system is so easy.

Here are some examples of malicious "insider attacks".

- **Collusion with Outsiders:** Insiders who steal or modify information are recruited by "outsiders", including organised crime.

↳ *Case Study: The Insider was a loan officer in a financial institution. The incident was part of a massive identity theft ring. They stole identities of at least 25 people and then used the identities to defraud other financial institutions and retailers for a total of $335,000. The ring leader was an outsider who carefully recruited participants, each with a specific role in the scheme. The crime occurred over a ten-month period.*

- **Business Partners:** A number of crimes are perpetrated by employees from trusted business partners who are given access to their clients' assets.

↳ *Case Study: The Insider was formerly employed as a contractor working for a telecommunications organisation as a software developer and tester. The person was terminated for poor performance. Unfortunately, he still had access to as many as 16 of his former employers' systems. The insider gained access to at least 24 accounts, read email, reviewed source code, and deleted some software modifications for a project.*

- **Mergers and Acquisitions:** Many insiders who commit malicious acts are individuals with a negative experience as the result of a merger or acquisition.

↳ *Case Study: A programmer in a logistic company was terminated due to a restructuring of the business. The organisation followed proper procedures by escorting him to his office to collect his belongings, and then escorting him out of the building. However, they overlooked one key password that was known to only three people within the organisation. The terminated Insider used that key password to gain access to the system that night and was able to delete the programs he had created while working there.*

- **Internet Underground:** Insiders using the Internet underground to collaborate, transact or even get assistance to commit their crime.

↳ *Case Study: A system administrator and several of his colleagues were laid off by a financial firm. Over a period of four days, after receiving the news, the Insider contacted management and threatened them. He stated; if he didn't receive a significantly larger severance package and good employment recommendations, he would recruit his friends from the Internet underground hacking ring to start attacking the organisation.*

Of course, not all insider incidents are the result of malicious intent. Many incidents are the result of human error. Often and without thinking of the potential consequences, users leave confidential documents in plain view, share passwords, circumvent security procedures, mishandle information, violate industry and government regulations, inadvertently dump data to the cloud, and lose laptops, USB's and/or other devices. The result of this "lack of care" can ultimately cost much more to your organisation's bottom line than the employee hoped to save in time.

According to a recent survey conducted by Ponemon Institute ("Closing Security Gaps to Protect Corporate Data: A Study of US and European Organizations" – August 2016), 50% of respondents said those who are most likely to cause compromise of Insider incidents are those that are negligent.

Question: Who is the most likely to cause the compromise of insider accounts within your organisation?

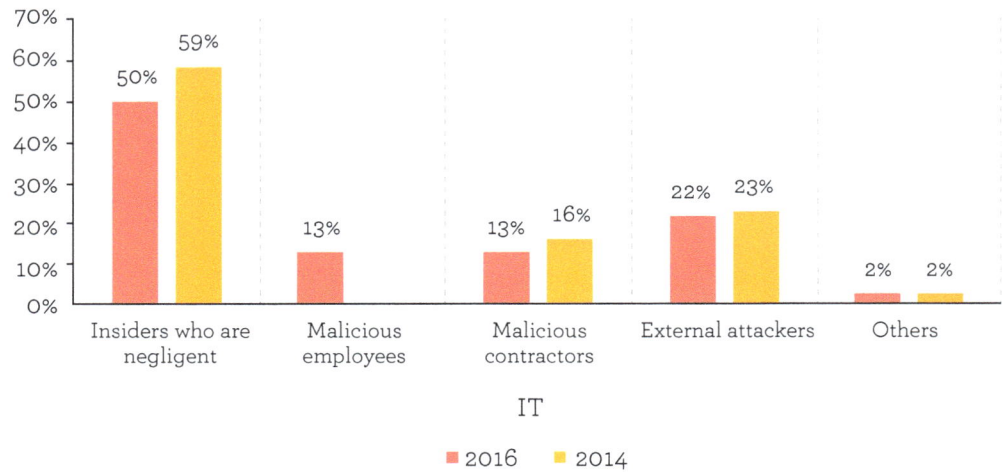

Bar chart:

Category	2016	2014
Insiders who are negligent	50%	59%
Malicious employees	13%	
Malicious contractors	13%	16%
External attackers	22%	23%
Others	2%	2%

IT

■ 2016 ■ 2014

HERE ARE SOME EXAMPLES

→ Personal details of several world leaders were accidently shared by the Australian Immigration Department before the G20 summit in November 2014. Passport numbers, dates of birth, and visa details of leaders attending the Brisbane summit were mistakenly emailed by a department official to a member of the Asian Cup Local Organising Committee.

→ In March 2016, Google suffered an embarrassing insider data breach after an employee at a third-party vendor mistakenly sent personal information (Social Security numbers and names) of an unspecified number of Mountain View employees to another company.

→ Uber accidentally exposed the personal data of hundreds of its drivers, revealing social security numbers, pictures of driver licenses, vehicle registration numbers and other information – October 2014.

→ Records of approximately 44,000 customers were inadvertently breached from the Federal Deposit Insurance Corp (FDIC) in February 2014. The breach occurred when a former employee accidentally downloaded the records to a personal device. The employee left on February 26, and the FDIC learned of the downloaded data three days later.

➥ In 2010, Microsoft accidentally leaked confidential data from its Cloud Services. The breach was linked to an unspecified "configuration issue" in Microsoft's data centres in the United States, Europe and Asia. The Offline Address Book component of Microsoft Business Productivity Online Suite (BPOS), which contains business contact information, was made available to non-authorised users.

➥ In 2014, Firefox maker Mozilla admitted it accidentally exposed the email addresses of almost 80,000 members of its Developer Network, along with thousands of encrypted passwords.

These examples lead me to conclude the following:

- Verizon 2015 Data Breach Investigation Report interestingly stated that 90% of all incidents are people, whether it's goofing up, getting infected, behaving badly, or losing stuff; and

- At this point, we need to own the problem. Take your index finger and point it to your chest, and proclaim "I am the problem".

YOUR BIGGEST RISKS ARE YOUR _____ INSIDERS

Q: The big question: How do you know whether you have an active Insider Threat right now?

A: You don't!

That's right, you have no idea! You have no inkling, visibility, or perception!

In the most likely case and with a high degree of certainty, you have an Insider actor prowling your organisation, and placing your assets at risk, right now!

And you don't even know it!

You have likely invested significantly in information security tools and processes, and capitalised a huge amount of resources and time to identify security risks and mitigation strategies in your organisation. You have likely spent a fortune on achieving compliance and governance regulations. And yet, your biggest threat is from inside your organisation where you invest the least.

According to a Gartner study, (Gartner is a leading IT and Technology advisory research firm) completed in 2015, **99% of the security budget is focused on external attacks.** This is a recipe for failure!

How can the National Security Agency (NSA) data breach by Edward Snowden and recently Martin Harold be explained- - - both individuals were trusted contractors. How is a breach of this magnitude possible, given the resources of the NSA, and other resources available to them?

72%
of Insider Threats are detected by non-technical people.

How can data breaches continue to occur within some of the largest businesses – Lockheed Martin; Target; Sony, AT&T, Fannie Mae, Morgan Stanley, Wells Fargo and many more?

The Insider Threat is always present, and if you think that your current set of security technologies, process and practices will protect your data and help mitigate these incidents, think again. ***"Around 72% of Insider Threats are detected by non-technical people"*** (The Cert Guide to Inside Threats. Moore, Cappelli, Trzeciak, 2012).

One of the classic quotes by Einstein is his definition of "insanity"...

"doing the same thing over and over again and expecting a different result".

Insiders Threats cannot be prevented and mitigated with technology alone.

This quote accurately describes current security practices and current thinking. If you realise just one thing, let it be this: ***"Insiders Threats cannot be prevented and mitigated with technology alone"***.

Insiders use authorised credentials to access systems and information every day to carry out their work. They have permission to access systems and information, and automated detection based solely on technology is extremely difficult and highly unlikely.

↳ Case Study: Wells Fargo fired 5,300 employees who created over 2 million phony accounts. Wells Fargo employees actually created phony PIN numbers and fake email addresses without customer knowledge, which enabled them to enrol customers in online banking services. In addition, fake credit card accounts were created. Wells Fargo was fined $185 million by the City of Los Angeles, and suffered the loss of some major projects as a result.

- The scandal cost Wells Fargo $30 Billion in investment activity with the State of Illinois.

- The City of Chicago is diverting $25 million of the City's investments from Wells Fargo & Co. The California State Treasurer made a similar announcement.

  The case clearly shows that when there is motivation, for example, a sales incentives program in place, fraudulent employees are able to work the system to their advantage bypassing security technologies that were put in place to protect the customer.

There is no doubt that security technology is improving, but technology alone is not enough. External based attacks are clearly where the majority of companies spend their security budget, as it is easier to detect and defend against these violations. However, these tools are seldom scalable or cost effective to apply with employees who require access to assets in order to do their job.

INSIDERS ARE A GATEWAY OF RISK

By definition, any person that has access to your corporate assets is a gateway of risk. Assets are defined as:
- People;
- Facilities;
- Systems; and
- Information.

People are mobile. There is no single person that works within the organisation facilities 100% of the time.

Every user goes home. and as soon as they leave the organisation premise, they become a "Gateway of Risk". Why? Because after work hours people are on their own time. They are free to access other environments, other systems, and other people, and the work organisation has no control over this time or these actions. In addition, 66% of employees tend to use their own personal device while at work (BYOD – Bring Your Own Device), which can complicate the circumstances further.

What this means is Insiders in your employ, can be influenced to exploit or even bypass your security controls either negligently or maliciously, and place your organisation at risk, as a result of a friendship or interaction with another individual.

It could also mean that outsiders can use your employees or contractors as a gateway to access those assets you protect so well.

↳ Case Study: On the night of Wednesday, August 27, 2003, two men dressed as computer technicians and carrying tool bags entered the cargo processing and intelligence centre at Sydney International Airport.

They presented themselves to the security desk as technicians sent by Electronic Data Systems, the outsourced customs computer services provider that regularly sends people to work on computers after office hours.

After supplying false names and signatures, they were given access to the top-security mainframe room, and they knew where to go. They spent two hours disconnecting two computers. They put them on trolleys and wheeled them past the security desk, into the lift and out of the building.

This case clearly shows that people (internal & external) are a serious risk to the organisation if not managed appropriately.

Here is an interesting quote:

"We Have To Start Addressing The Human Element Of Information Security, Not Just The Technical. It's Only Then, We Will Stop Being The Punching Bag!"

(Centre for Strategic Studies in the Crossfire: Critical Infrastructure in the Age of Cyber War, 2009).

THE
TRUSTED
USER

_____

How much trust do you place in your colleagues? Do you know every employee in your organisation personally?

How is a person deemed trustworthy?

Does trusting your boss leave you vulnerable?

HERE IS AN EXAMPLE ──────────────

➡ The Enron scandal, revealed in October 2001, eventually led to the bankruptcy of the Enron Corporation. It came about because Enron executives used accounting loopholes, special purpose entities, and poor financial reporting to hide billions of dollars in debt from failed deals and projects.

What about trusting your co-workers, or employees? Here is an example.

➡ A former employee at a bank in Queenstown, New Zealand was convicted and imprisoned after being found guilty of stealing more than $400,000 from her employer. Investigators found that she began committing her inside-attack against the bank in 2010 and continued until 2013. She created sixteen fictitious accounts with loans and overdrafts ranging from $12,000 to $120,000. Altogether, the amount stolen totalled $402,386.

Once a person is selected to become an employee of an organisation, that employee is granted "automatic" level of trust within the organisation. This does not mean, that the person is granted full physical and information access to sensitive assets, but it does imply that the new employee is granted a high level of trust from other colleagues.

Trust is human nature. It is one of our driving needs to connect. We want to connect to one another – it's a "human" need. That's why Facebook & LinkedIn go out of their way to recommend new Friends/Contacts from your trusted circle of friends/contacts.

An organisation is a "social invention" for accomplishing common goals. As such, organisations have people who present both opportunities and risks.

How easy is it to breach someone's trust?

It's simple. For example, to set up a phony ID on any social networking site, you could accomplish the following.

➦ Request to be 'friends' with a dozen strangers on LinkedIn. Perhaps half of them accept. Collect a list of all their connections.

➦ Go to Facebook and search for those six people. Perhaps you find four of them also on Facebook. Request to be their friends on Facebook. All accept because you're already an established friend in LinkedIn.

➦ With those two people that are not on Facebook, you could setup a fake but convincing user profile on Facebook by grabbing their information from LinkedIn and posting it in Facebook. Then you could use these two users to send 'friend' requests to your victims on Facebook and there you have it.

➦ And as a bonus, Facebook itself will suggest to you other friends to those people and the probability is that they will accept to be your friend. Think about the trust factor here. For these secondary victims, they not only feel they know you, but actually request 'friend' status. They sought you out.

Now, imagine what you can ask from a person who is your 'friend'?

THE
EQUATION
OF TRUST

According to Stephen Covey, the author of *"The Speed Of Trust"* book, TRUST is a function of two key variables.

· **Character.** Character is based on Integrity, Motives and Intent.

· **Competence.** Competence is based on Capabilities, Skills and Results.

You might think a person is sincere and honest, but you won't trust them if they are not able to produce results. This is typified by politicians; they have an abundance of intent, but rarely deliver results. Politicians rarely "walk their talk" as the saying goes. That is why their trust levels are so low.

Another person might have great skills and a good track record, but if they don't show integrity or humility, then they are not likely to be trusted. This is typified by business people who thrive on power at the expense of others.

When a person gets interviewed and hired for employment, predominantly, it's their competence that gets assessed – Their resume, their skills, their experience, their certifications and references are all evaluated.

And yet the character of the person very rarely gets appraised. Why? Because, evaluating character is extremely difficult and expensive.

Each person is unique with their own set of values, beliefs, thoughts, philosophies, likes and dislikes.

No matter how much you trust someone, it's always a good idea to verify the trust. Your most trusted employees are the ones with the most opportunity to steal, defraud, bend the rules or divulge information accidentally.

Need I say more? Just remember the example provided by Edward Snowdens' behaviour.

HUMANS ARE NOT MACHINES

Insiders are people, not computers. Treating Insiders as a technology problem ignores the human aspects of motivation and behaviour.

People have emotions, a conscience, hopes, values, beliefs and dreams.

People need to feel respected, want a sense of belonging, and need recognition for their contributions. People need autonomy, personal growth, and meaning in their work.

When these criteria are met, the work relationship is enriching for both the organisation and the employee. When they are not met, it drains significant energies and affects the dynamics of both sides.

When people relate to one another in ways that fail to reflect shared values, the result is a dysfunctional relationship.

By and large, individuals are more than their behaviours. Most often, however, we do not separate individuals from their behaviours.

Let's look at it this way:

BELIEF + VALUES **ATTITUDE** **BEHAVIOUR** **RESULT**

- **Beliefs and values** set a person's framework to their **Attitude.**

- Activities are influenced based on a person's **Attitude**, and that leads to a specific **Behaviour**, which produces a specific **Result**.

In our everyday business life, we frequently try and change the behaviour of others, in an effort to achieve a certain Result. For example:

- Behaviour towards ethical business practice;

- Behaviour towards anticipated changes, such as an introduction of new technology; or

- Behaviour about security and safety practices.

In organisations, management place considerable focus on how to enhance productivities via changing behaviours. They focus on high performance, by giving training or mentoring programs that are behavioural based. When the training or mentoring program ends, the behaviours normally change back to what they were.

Why does it change back? Why isn't it long lasting? Because, behaviour is only a result of the frames (thoughts, values and beliefs), that drive it.

When organisations try to engage in the Behaviour of people, and the behaviour desired by the organization is not aligned with the "frames" of the people, the result is stress, tension, frustration, and eventually anger.

The more organisations try to plug people into specific security controls, and influence/ manage/mandate behaviours and operations, the more stress results.

"Stress" can have a huge impact on organisation viability. In the last decade, stress has become a serious concern for individuals as well as organisations.

The level of stress in the workplace is at all time high and the implications of this should be cause for wide-ranging concerning.

Research has found that stress can cause heart diseases, ulcers, memory loss, immune deficiency, and greater vulnerability to infections. Illness leads to negative consequences for organisations, for example, lower productivity, increase in non-malicious human errors, higher rates of turnover, worker conflicts, increase in worker's compensation to possible business sabotage, theft or fraud.

According to the Insider Threat division of CERT (Software Engineering Institute | Carnegie Mellon University), who compiled more than a thousand Insider Threat cases, stress is a huge key factor behind Insider Threats incidents.

The following table demonstrates the stages of burnout and their symptoms (I have borrowed some of the ideas from "Organisation Behaviour – Understanding and Managing Life at Work" by Gary Johns and Alan M. Saks)

EMOTIONAL EXHAUSTION	DEPERSONALISATION	LOW PERSONAL ACCOMPPLISHMENTS	AGRIEVED
↪ Feel drained	↪ Treats people like objects	↪ Cannot deal with people	↪ Argues
↪ Feel fatigued	↪ Doesn't care what happens	↪ Cannot understand others	↪ Not punctual
↪ Frustrated	↪ Feels that other blame for their problems	↪ Cannot emphasize with others	↪ Angry
↪ Flustered	↪ Highly irritated	↪ Doesn't want to work	↪ Abusive
			↪ Threatening

For organisations that are seeking to drive security and resilience into operations, they must understand and acknowledge that each individual person is unique. Failure to take into account the frames of each individual person, will usually lead to tears in personal affairs.

EMPLOYERS ARE NOT PARENTS

One of the biggest costs to organisations is the "disengaged employee". According to Gallup, http://www.gallup.com/poll/188144/employee-engagement-stagnant-2015.aspx, on average, 70% of the workforce are disengaged in some aspect with the work they are performing, and the level of disengagement hasn't changed much over the past ten years.

A disengaged employee can be recognised by a number of signs, however if you really stop and consider each employee, you should be able to recognise those who are working for the benefit of the business, and differentiate them from those who are solely focused on themselves. The Gallup study report values the annual cost of disengagement between $450 and $550 Billion in the US alone.

A disengaged employee may lack initiative, use social media in a manner that is noticeable, lack enthusiasm, complain a lot, fail to interact, fail to be a team member, fail to be proactive, often fail in achieving milestones, and happily places blame on others.

A disengaged employee may pose a threat to the organisation. Why? The possibility ranges from a lack of productivity, to letting things 'slide', to harming the organisation by deceitful or malicious behaviour.

A disengaged employee at the extreme end poses the greatest threat to the organisation as an 'insider actor'. They are a security threat, and their actions range from disregarding security policy up to actively stealing information and possibly sabotaging critical systems.

It is important to realise that leaders and executives who are personally involved in the business, and able to recognise and acknowledge the achievements of their employees, are more likely to have engaged employees working for the benefit of their business.

First, office culture starts with the leader. A leader who actively encourages a sense of community and team spirit, and fosters team relationships, may help prevent an employee from becoming disenchanted and antisocial within the team environment.

Second, direct managers play a massive role in fostering healthy downstream relationships. However, most organisations today support direct managers who focus their energy on maintaining upstream and side-stream relationships.

Having said that, leaders are the number one reason employees quit their job.

Business leaders are not parents, nor should they be. Yet, there is a strong causative relationship between the line manager behaviour and employee engagement levels.

The key to employee engagement is not parenting, but nurturing. By nurturing, I mean showing interest in the employee and their lives beyond work; focusing on strengths;

listening generously; speaking straight; providing regular informal feedback and recognition; and holding team members accountable.

The bottom line is that executives struggle to practice behaviours like these, and at the same time, they are exceedingly busy. It is difficult for executives to engender employee engagement when they are unable to slow down and take control of their schedule, and focus on the "Important" but not "Urgent". When they get control of their time, they can focus on what is really important, reducing the likelihood of an employee going rogue and ultimately placing the organisation at risk.

HOW TO USE THIS BOOK?

Where to start?

You can always read the book from Start to Finish, but this book is not a novel and what I really want you to do is focus on a key area that may address a specific issue or a challenge that you may be experiencing regarding Insider Threats.

Having said that, here are some suggestions.

1. If you just want a casual overview of the insider threat landscape, start with the **Seven Potential Signs That You May Already Be Compromised** *that* follows this chapter.

2. If you have some Insider Threat concerns and want to address that, start with the **Checklist Questionnaire**, and then follow up with the **Seven Potential Signs That You May Be Already Compromised**. This will provide you with some context.

3. If you have suffered an Insider Threat incident, and want some advice on best practices, approach one of the specific areas of the **Seven Potential Signs That You May Be Already Compromised** and follow the recommendations or contact CommsNet Group.

4. Alternatively, feel free to browse the book as it is filled with information you may not know you don't know!

SEVEN POTENTIAL SIGNS THAT YOU MAY ALREADY BE COMPROMISED

Is your organisation compromised? Do you have an insider that is placing your organisation at risk right now? If you are employing people, then the answer is "Yes".

How does this relate to you? Should any of the following seven signs be TRUE, this would most likely indicate that your organisation is already compromised by an Insider Actor.

1. **You Are Unable To Enforce Corporate Policies**

2. **You Have Not Integrated Insider Risks as Part of Your Enterprise Risk Management Plan**

3. **You Are Unaware Of Negative Behaviour in the Workplace**

4. **You Are Unable To Rigorously Manage Identity and Access Controls**

5. **You Don't Have Real Time System and Data Behaviour Anomaly Detection**

6. **You Don't Have Real Time User Behaviour Anomaly Detection**

7. **You Haven't Instituted An Insider Threat Program**

- 1 -
YOU ARE UNABLE TO ENFORCE CORPORATE POLICIES

Every organisation tries to formalise its working ecosystem aspect through policies. These policies define what is expected, and also describe how non-compliance is dealt with.

So, when a new employee joins the organisation, they customarily receive a copy of the organisation employee handbook that clearly lays out what is expected of them and the associated consequences.

Even though every employee has read and agreed to the policies/terms, an organisation has no way of knowing whether these policies have been understood, effectively absorbed, or whether they are followed.

Keeping these policies updated and ensuring that everyone has access to, and is aware of the changes in those policies is complex, and the complexity increases as the number of employees and work locations increase.

The biggest challenge for any organisation is not knowing whether their policies are being enforced.

Sure, organisations can run regular training and awareness programs, but if the program is not run on a weekly basis, it doesn't become a habit. When it doesn't become a habit, it is not part of the culture, and people make mistakes. After all, we are human.

Secondly, employees forget, and may find it difficult to follow policies if they are not coherent. Clear and consistent enforced policies will certainly reduce the likelihood that an employee will feel unfairly treated.

Employees are more likely to correctly and consistently follow policies that are:

- Clearly articulated.

  o They are precise;

  o They are concise; and

  o They are coherent.

- Consistently enforced.

- Available for reference as well as circulated and refreshed.

- Include reasoning behind the policies and the ramification of policy violation.

WHAT ARE YOUR VULNERABILITIES?

➡ **You do not have specific policies that address Insider Threats.**
If you fail to include specific policies that outline Insider policy violations, then you plan to fail.

➡ **You have no way of knowing whether your policies are being enforced in real time or not.**
This is probably the most difficult challenge that organisations face today, and this, by itself, can leave you completely vulnerable to an insider breach.

➡ **Senior Management and Executives do not comply with organisation policies.**
If management does not set the example by complying with policies, subordinates see this as a sign that policies do not matter, or that not all employees are held to the same standard.

➡ **Policies are not reviewed or tested.**
Whenever workforce regards policies as restrictions that make little or no sense, or they are simply too difficult to understand, they are ignored. Remember, organisations are not static, and as they grow and improve, all policies must be reviewed to ensure that they are serving the organisation well.

➡ **Poor policy development and approach.**
Forgetting the motto of the KISS principle (Keep it Simple and Smart). Some policies, are just too complex, too long, too onerous and politically convoluted.

➡ **Social Media is left in the hands of the employees.**
Insiders who use social media sites can intentionally or unintentionally threaten organisation assets. For example, social media allows people to easily share personal information about themselves with others, such as, birthdates, details of their address, likes, hobbies, family members, and business affiliations. Posting this information publicly exposes social media users to possible social engineering attack.

↳ Case Study: A government agency employed a lead software engineer whose team was developing a software suite. After a number of major issues with the development of the software, the employee learned that the agency was going to outsource future development.

The employee filed a grievance and took a leave of absence. The agency denied the grievance, so the employee resigned. However, prior to resigning, the employee copied the source code, encrypting it and placing it on removable media, then deleted the source code from his laptop, which he turned in at the time of his resignation. He explained that he had intentionally deleted the source code as part of "wiping" his laptop before turning it in, but did not disclose that he retained a copy.

The organisation discovered that he had deleted the only copy of the source code. The system running the code was still able to function, although they could not fix any bugs or make any enhancements.

Investigators managed to discover that he had copied the software at his home. After nine months, the insider finally admitted his actions and provided the cryptographic key.

In this case, the organisation had poor policies and procedures for software development. The organisation should have held all software, and the incident may have been avoided completely. In addition, a change management process that captures changes to code throughout development should have been in place, especially because the software was used in a mission critical system. This type of structured control ensures that someone in addition to the lead software engineer has access to a copy of the source code.

RECOMMENDATION - WHAT YOU NEED TO DO:

1. Develop policies and procedures that specifically address Insider Threats.
If appropriate, involve the policy and procedures development team within your organisation.

2. As mentioned, policies and controls need to be consistent, precise and coherent.
The least knowledgeable employee must be able to understand and follow them with ease.

3. Policies must be adopted by all including executives and management.
Executive support and adoption is crucial as discussed in Point 7 – *"Institute Insider Threat Program"*. Leaders must set/be the example for employees.

4. Policies and controls need to be revaluated on a regular basis.
You need to understand which policies work and which don't.

- If a policy is never breached, it is probably because it is too difficult to trip. This could signify that the policy may not be written correctly.

- If the policy is breached often, this may indicate a lack of understanding and education by employees, and it may need to be reviewed.

5. Use of a sophisticated *User Behaviour Monitoring Solution* that monitors what users are doing and whether they are violating any of your corporate policies and controls in real time. This is described in more detail in Section 6 – *"Institute User Behaviour Monitoring"*.

The key here is the ongoing educating and notification to employees when they breach policies in real time. Think of it like this. When kids misbehave, you direct them a warning. You continue to direct warnings, with increasing severity, until they understand and recognise the consequences. This is, by far, the most effective way to shape human behaviour.

Should an employee be warned for violating their organisation policy, he or she will learn not to perform that same action.

Should a malicious person be warned of their actions, this person will realise that he or she is being monitored and therefore, will not continue with that activity.

6. Establish a social media policy that defines acceptable use of social media and information that should not be discussed online.

- Include social media awareness training.

- Monitor social media activities.

- 2 -
YOU HAVE NOT INTEGRATED INSIDER RISKS AS PART OF YOUR ENTERPRISE RISK MANAGEMENT PLAN

All organisations operate under the shadow of risk. The purpose of a risk management program is to identify, analyse and control risk to the organisation assets.

A risk management program usually involves:

• Identifying high value or critical assets; and

• Assessing the potential types and frequency of threats or risk against those assets.

It is not practical for organisations to implement 100% protection against every threat. However, it is important to focus on protecting those assets that are deemed critical to the mission from both external and internal threats.

Risk is the combination of threat, vulnerability and mission impact. Enterprise wide risk assessment helps identify critical assets, potential threats to those assets, and mission impact if the assets are compromised.

Unfortunately, many organisations focus solely on protecting information from access or sabotage by those external to the organisation, and overlook the Insider Threat.

For example, most organisations rely on some technical security solution designed without consciously acknowledging and accounting for, the potential Insider Threat. This leaves the role of protection in the hands of those that may be the potential threat – Yes, the Insiders themselves.

WHAT ARE YOUR VULNERABILITIES?

➡ **Insider Threat are NOT treated as a category of risk.** Failing to recognise the potential threat from Insiders, leaves the organisation completely vulnerable.

➡ **Insider Risks are very rarely assessed, if at all.** Failing to assess the state of the organisation or failing to prepare against the Insider Threat leaves the organisation completely exposed to severe impacts – Loss of Intellectual property; Loss of Income; Loss of Reputation; and Loss of Business.

➡ **Insider threats are not discussed at senior management briefings and meetings.** Failing to get management and executive support and agreement that Insider Threat is important also leaves the organisation wide open for massive damages.

↳ *Case Example: A computer system attendant employed by a Government contractor created fake Government email addresses on the Government systems for which he was responsible. He then used those email addresses to request replacement parts for equipment recalled by a major supplier. The supplier sent the replacement parts to the address specified in the emails, with the understanding that the "faulty" parts would be returned after the replacement had been received. The insider provided his home address for the shipment and never intended to return the original equipment. He received almost 100 shipments with a retail value of $5 million and sold the equipment on the Internet.*

The incident points out the need for transaction verification to be built into the supplier purchase agreements. Even though operations may be outsourced, safeguards still need to be built into those operations as part of the enterprise risk assessment, to ensure that trusted business partners implement adequate controls against Insider Threats.

RECOMMENDATIONS - WHAT YOU NEED TO DO:

1. **To make better informed decisions about risks, senior management must understand the risk posed by Insiders.** Insider Threats are risks that need to be treated as a category of risk and managed as part of your enterprise risk management process.

   - Identify high-value or critical assets;

   - Assess the potential types and frequency of threat or risks that insiders may perform against those assets (whether malicious or unintentional);

   - Determine the approach for addressing those risks; and

   - Deal with each risk by implementing its defined control plan or accept the risk.

2. **Insider risks must be evaluated at least once a year.**

3. **Discuss Insider Threats at senior management risk briefings and meetings.**

- 3 -
YOU ARE UNAWARE OF NEGATIVE BEHAVIOUR IN THE _____ WORKPLACE

As organisations are a collection of people who share a common purpose and unite to focus their various skills and achieve specific goals, it makes sense that they also pose the biggest threat to the organisation.

What makes a person with a "good background" behave appallingly towards colleagues, while another with "little resource" bends backwards to help people?

One thing is clear, humans are not random creatures. Everything we do, we do for a reason and often with intention. There is a force that drives us. What is this force that is controlling our lives, at this moment? Pain - Pleasure. Everything that you and I do, we do either out of a need to avoid pain or a desire to gain pleasure. The question arises... why would a person behave in a manner that could jeopardise their employers' organisation, and put it at risk? The answer is simple; at some level, they believe that taking action at that moment will result in pleasure, and that pleasure will be greater than the pain that may result if caught.

Below are examples of Human Behaviour; some that can't be observed by the employer because they occur outside the work environment, and some that are observed in the work environment.

Negative Background Behaviour (Unobserved)	Negative Observed Behavior at Work
Personal Disposition	Conflicts with Colleagues
Mental health Disorders	Aggressive Behaviour
Social Skills Challenges	Violent Behaviour
History of Rule Violations	Mood Swings
Criminal Behaviour	Bizarre Behaviour
Addicted Gambler	Poor Performance
Addicted Drug Use	Absence
Financial Difficulties	Sexual Harassment
Going Through Nasty Divorce	Poor Hygiene
Physical Abusive	Misuse of Corporate Resources

Individuals with a negative background behaviour usually display the behaviour in some form in the work environment.

There is a strong link between negative background behaviour and the empirical evidence that the Insider *Threat Division of CERT concluded during their study of over 1,000 Insider Threat incidents.* **In their study, each incident of IT Sabotage was performed by an individual who exhibited a personal disposition.**

What is Personal Disposition? It is a characteristic linked to a propensity to exhibit malicious insider behaviour. This might explain why one employee ends up attacking an organisation while other co-workers do not.

WHAT ARE YOUR VULNERABILITIES?

➡ **Supervisors and managers pay little attention to negative workplace behaviour, and sometimes they even ignore complaints.** This establishes a dangerous situation and even sets a precedence for employees to vent their frustrations causing negative morale and lack of trust within the working environment. Unfortunately, in many Insider incidents, the concerning behaviours are not recognised or dealt with appropriately by management before an incident occurs.

➡ **Most insiders who commit IT Sabotage are disgruntled due to unmet expectations.** Serious unmet expectations may cause employees to seek revenge and result in serious Insider incidents, especially if the disgruntled insider has a personal disposition.

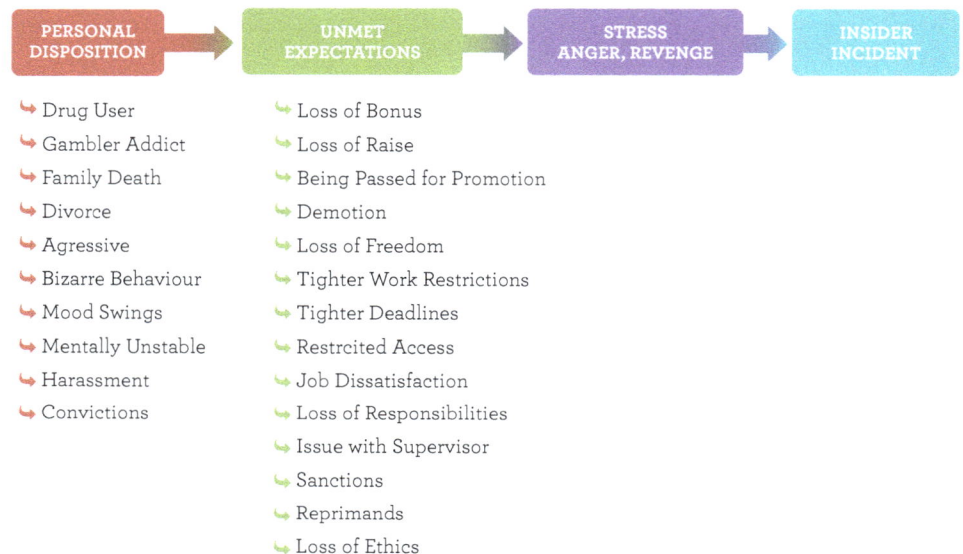

PERSONAL DISPOSITION	UNMET EXPECTATIONS	STRESS ANGER, REVENGE	INSIDER INCIDENT

↳ Drug User	↳ Loss of Bonus
↳ Gambler Addict	↳ Loss of Raise
↳ Family Death	↳ Being Passed for Promotion
↳ Divorce	↳ Demotion
↳ Agressive	↳ Loss of Freedom
↳ Bizarre Behaviour	↳ Tighter Work Restrictions
↳ Mood Swings	↳ Tighter Deadlines
↳ Mentally Unstable	↳ Restrcited Access
↳ Harassment	↳ Job Dissatisfaction
↳ Convictions	↳ Loss of Responsibilities
	↳ Issue with Supervisor
	↳ Sanctions
	↳ Reprimands
	↳ Loss of Ethics

➡ **Inconsistent application of policies.** Senior management and executives do not follow and comply with organisation policies. If management and executives do not respect and comply with policies, subordinates will see this as a sign that policies do not matter, or suspect that they are being held to a different standard. In addition, failure to define and enforce policies consistenly can result in cases where employees are emboldened to commit repeated violations that escalate in severity, causing significant harm to the organisation.

➡ **Organisation doesn't have an Employee Assistance Program.** Without the ability to proactively provide ongoing assistance, counselling services, and general caring for the well-being of employees regarding their personal or work related issues, your organisation will most likely experience a change in job performance, in morale, in behaviour, in trust, and in the overall engagement of personnel within the organisation.

For example: As managers observe ongoing negative behaviour by an employee as a result of business restructuring, they should consider providing positive intervention to lower / decrease disgruntlement.

➡ **Ongoing education and awareness training around Insider Threats not provided.** According to the Insider Threat Division of CERT, around 72% of Insider Incidents have been discovered by non-technical people. A lack of training reduces the effectiveness of your users and their ability to identify suspicious workplace behaviour. Training could increase employee ability to identify negative behaviour, and reduce the impact and harm committed by Insiders.

➡ **Ineffective employee termination process.** A lax termination process can increase the opportunity for an Insider Threat to take place especially for a disgruntled person who may be seeking revenge. There are countless cases where a departed employee was still able to gain access into the organisation many months after they departed.

↳ *Case Example : Reports spread within an organisation that the annual bonus would be substantially smaller than usual. This prompted a system administrator to begin constructing a logic bomb from home. He then propagated the logic bomb to the company's network servers as part of the standard server upgrade. He resigned when he found out the rumours were true. The logic bomb, which he had set to go off two weeks later, deleted billions of files and disrupted services on thousands of systems throughout the United States.*

RECOMMENDATION - WHAT YOU NEED TO DO:

1. Build an effective trustworthy workforce for your organisation.
- A trustworthy workforce begins with determining TRUST prior to hiring an individual, and

- Continues by applying regular screening mechanisms to the workforce, based upon position within the organisation, or the need for access to critical assets.

2. "See Something – Say Something". There needs to be a mechanism for employees and affiliates to confidentiality report suspicious activities based on specific indicators, or potential malicious insider activity, or facts with evidence of wrong doing.

3. Develop Insider Threat Promotional Materials such as posters, magnets, login banners, etc. Increase awareness through distribution and posting promotional material, and use it to keep employee awareness high regarding Insider Threats. You may also want to publish or share "Real-Life Experiences" in forums such as:
- Periodic seminar or case studies that cover Insider Threats;

- Lunch and Learn sessions;

- Newsletters with tips and reminders;

- Talks by senior management or even outside experts;

- Session to review your "Acceptable use agreement"; and

- Internal website where employees can find reference material, training, and other information about Insider Threats.

4. Insider Threat training for all employees. Implement an awareness training program that is conducted on a regular basis. It may include the following:
- The type of threats;

- How employees may be targeted;

- Unintentional Insider Threats and what they are;

- How to identify inappropriate behaviour;

- Responsibilities of employees to report incidents;

- The importance of engaging all employees to prevent malicious Insider activities; and

- How to report threats or incidents.

5. Management & Supervisor Training. Training for Management and Supervisors may include the following:
- Identify potential behaviour precursors and understand where and how to refer or handle such situations;

- Identify employees under stress and help them get the right counselling or assistance;

- Assess trustworthiness of employees before assigning them critical duties;

- Understand the key critical assets and mission of the organisation; and

- Understand what is considered "abnormal behaviour".

6. Implement an Employee Assistance Program. Employee Assistance Programs (EAP) help employees deal with personal or work related issues that may affect job performance, health, and general well-being. An EAP may include:
- Counselling services for employees; and

- It can be used to handle employee disgruntlement and serve as positive intervention.

7. Develop a comprehensive employee termination procedure. Your procedure should include the following:
- Create a checklist to use when someone separates from your organisation, and always use it;

- Reaffirm with the departed employee any agreements about IP and nondisclosures;

- Archive and block all access to all accounts associated with the departed employee;

- Collect all of the departing employees company owned assets prior to leaving;

- Disable remote access and any remote management capabilities. Change passwords of all shared accounts. Disable mobile devices so they are unable to access your corporate information; and

- Apply the above processes to all trusted business partners.

- 4 -
YOU ARE UNABLE TO RIGOROUSLY MANAGE IDENTITY AND ACCESS CONTROLS

By definition, system administrators and privileged users have greater access to systems, networks or applications than other users. The perception is that these privileged users pose an increased risk because:

- They have the technical ability and access to perform malicious actions; and

- They can usually conceal their actions by using their privileges to falsify their activities.

However, system administrators and privileged users make up approximately 5% of the organisation employees, and that is not a large amount. Let us not forget that the remaining 95% of employees still have access to other critical assets.

According to the Insider Threat division of CERT, *"75% of Insider Theft of IP (Intellectual Property) already had authorised access to the information"*. But that doesn't mean that they should have had access. In many organisations, employees tend to accumulate privileges needed to perform their job, and as they move into new roles through career progression, access they no longer need is not removed.

Insiders that steal IP are usually current employees. Based on the thousands of Insider Threat cases that the Insider Threat division of CERT identified, *"there isn't a single instance where a system administrator stole IP"*. This doesn't mean that it doesn't happen. What it does convey, is that we are spending a huge amount of money, time, and energy, on potentially unnecessary security controls.

75%
of Insider Theft of IP (Intellectual Property) had already authorised access to the information.

WHAT ARE YOUR VULNERABILITIES?

➡ **No matter how vigilant your organisation is against attackers, if an organisation account is compromised by an Outsider, that Outsider is NOW an Insider.** Most smart attackers move from machine to machine and gain greater access and privilege to higher value data inside the organisation. This approach provides the attacker additional points of control in a compromised network. The presence of "lateral movement" is a clear indicator of a threat that is attempting to extend its reach and control.

Once inside, they can do irreparable harm resulting in damaged reputations, financial losses, stolen data and loss of intellectual property.

➡ **You do not have the ability to "see" or "manage" or "control" access to your systems real time.** In order to keep your assets secure, you need to ensure that the right people have the right access at the right time. You must account for those people that join (new to the organisation), and those that leave the organisation, as well as those users who change roles as their time with the organisation increases. It's often found that as employees grow and move to new positions within an organisation, they accrue access to different systems as it becomes necessary for them to perform each different role.

For example, organisations have little if any visibility into whether unauthorised back door accounts have been created. Back doors accounts can provide an employee, an ex-employee, or even unauthorised 3rd party, access to the organisation system and information.

➡ **You have no strict procedures and controls on enforcing "least" privilege access.** Organisations have little real time visibility into which accounts have privileges or which accounts have administration rights. For example, granting too much access to users, whether it is at too deep of a level or for too many systems, is an issue that many organisations face. And, "entitlement creep" creates easy traps into which you can fall. All it takes is for one person with the wrong set of access controls to cause a disaster and mayhem.

➡ **You are using shared accounts for critical systems.** For example, an insider that has resigned or was terminated, may still be able to access remotely through this shared account, not to mention, when using shared accounts, users are able to hide their ill activities. What I mean is if there is no "separation of duties" on key processes, this may allow Insiders to conduct malicious activities without being identified.

➡ **You have no defined credentials and authentication management.** When many different systems are employed by an organisation, employees manage their own passwords to those systems and this can be confusing, complicated, and manually challenging. The lack of seamless provisioning, granting, and revoking across multiple applications leaves the organisation vulnerable.

➡ **You have no defined password requirements.** Poor password practices and policies make the organisation extremely vulnerable to be hacked. For example, employees sharing their passwords with others; Employees not locking their console screen before stepping away; Employees leaving sticky notes with their password attached to their screen for all to see; and Employees choosing very easy guessable passwords such as "123456", "password" or "qwerty".

➡ **You do not enforce separation of duties and least privileges.** Without the ability to divide specific functions amongst a number of people, you limit the possibility that a single employee could steal information, commit fraud or sabotage without the cooperation or knowledge of others. For example, a payroll officer could create a fictitious employee, pay this employee, and then remove this employee from the system without anyone finding out.

➡ **You have "Untracked staff".** Contractors often bypass HR when entering an organisation and as such, they are not tracked through HR or any centralised system. In the event that there is a breach or data is compromised, HR is unable to take any action because they have no awareness, or knowledge of the third party.

➡ **You have "Lingering Post-Contractor Access".** Contractors have access to systems and sensitive data that continues after termination because there is no formal process for severing access. Adding to this risk is the fact that contractors move around from organisation to organisation, sometimes working multiple contracts at the same time. If they jump to a competitor, lingering access could be potentially catastrophic.

↳ *Case Example : A contractor was formerly employed as a software developer and tester for the organisation. The organisation terminated his employment due to poor performance but failed to change a shared account password upon his departure. The ex-contractor was able to remotely access his former organisation ignoring warning signs of criminal violations. The Insider exploited 13 systems storing trade secrets valued at approximately $1.3 million.*

This case illustrates failure in user account management practices. This case includes a failure to realise a change in employee status, failure in ability to suspend or delete the account, failure to realise shared access accounts membership, and failure to identify remote access permission.

RECOMMENDATIONS - WHAT YOU NEED TO DO:

1. It is suggested by the Australian Signals Directorate (ASD), that business follow the Top 4 Mitigation Strategies to Mitigate Against Cyber Intrusion
🏠 http://www.asd.gov.au/infosec/mitigationstrategies.htm

- According to ASD, at least 85% of the targeted cyber intrusions could have been prevented by following the Top 4 mitigation strategies.

- Having said that, ASD released the Essential Eight Strategies to Mitigate Cyber Security Essentials.
🏠 https://www.asd.gov.au/publications/protect/essential-eight-explained.htm

2. Implement Next Generation End Point protection. The ability to proactively and continuously protect against everyday threats, as well as sophisticated attacks that are undetectable and invisible to traditional Anti-Virus (AV) solutions is critical.

- Do you know whether your organisation is owned? How do you know whether an Outsider is not an Insider right now? According to Ponemon Institute, *it takes 170 days to detect an advanced attack, 39 days to contain it, and 43 days to remediate it.* You need to take your End Point protection to the next level.

3. Develop a "User and Identity Governance" practice. The foundation of any "access" risk management approach should be adherence to the principles of least privilege access. It should include the following:

- Discover and profile all known and unknown assets, shared accounts, user accounts, and service accounts to gain control of credentials throughout the organisation.

- Develop a central place to model roles, policies, risk, and business process including enabling business users to manage access to any device, system or application.

- Perform regular audits of user entitlements. For example, if your users can assign excess entitlements to new roles, this may create segregation of duties violations as well as other business risks.

- Remove orphaned accounts. For example, if your organisation termination procedures are lax, former employees may still retain some or all of the access entitlements.

- Enforce least privileges. Remove permissions that are not needed.

- Ensure employees cannot perform critical functions without oversight and approval.

- Identify privilege accounts abuse. Detect administer-level privileges used in improper ways.

- Identify shared accounts and 1) shut them down, or 2) add a secondary identification. Even the best employees share credentials when they know that they should not, and this gives rise to separation-of-duties violation and "finger pointing".

- Monitor user actions so that organisations can detect access including 3rd party misuse of credentials that is in violation of policy--do all this in real time.

- Ensure users can be authenticated appropriately and establish if authentication, reissuance, and revocation policies are incurring more risk than deemed acceptable.

- Have an aggressive clean-up of access. During employee ongoing activities and upon termination of an employee or a contractor, it is critical to ensure that the organisation clean up the access environment at the individual application and entitlement level for the person.

At least **85%** of the targeted cyber intrusions could have been prevented by following the Top 4 mitigation strategies.

4. Develop a "Data Governance" practice.
You need to have the visibility of knowing where your key data assets are, so that you can effectively manage and protect the data.

- Where is your sensitive data and where is it exposed?

- Who has access to it and who should not?

- Who does it belong to?

- Who is using it at any moment in time?

- Who will be impacted if changes occur to this data?

- How can you tell if your data is secure and "living" in the right location?

Consider these three key management areas.

1. Reduce the likelihood of insider's exfiltrating data out of your organisation, such as copying data onto physical media: CD-ROMs, DVD-ROMs, laptops, USB drives, smartphones, tablets or other portable devices.

2. Reduce the risk that insiders may introduce their own devices which might harbour malware software, or uploading their previous job data onto your network.

3. Reduce the risk of Shadow IT where workers and departments either build or install their preferred applications and programmes onto corporate devices and systems without the permission or the awareness of the organisation.

- 5 -

YOU DON'T HAVE REAL TIME SYSTEM AND DATA BEHAVIOUR ANOMALY DETECTION

Security controls are defined by NIST 800-53A, as the "management, operational and technical safeguards or countermeasures prescribed for an information system to protect the confidentiality, integrity, and availability of the system and information."

However, the variety of compromises that rely on unauthorised modifications to victim's organisation assets, suggest the need for stronger change controls, as well as the ability to be alerted by system anomalies.

For example, many malicious Insiders have made unauthorised modifications to the organisation systems such as inserting backdoors, changing application code, or modifying databases. Unfortunately, most organisations struggle because they do not have the ability to see that there has been some critical change within their environment, not to mention the ability to mitigate the problem before it is too late.

Every organisation has a unique network topology characteristic such as bandwidth utilisation, usage patterns, and protocols that can be monitored for anomalies and changes. Deviations from normal behaviour can signal possible security incidents.

The ability to detect network and system irregularities is now essential in the battle against advanced malware, and also against an administrator who may have misconfigured a system making it extremely vulnerable for attack.

Anomalies also extend to business operations. For example, an abundance of Skype traffic in the network used by your inside sales team is probably a normal part of operations. However, if the database server that houses your customer list suddenly shows a burst of Skype traffic something is likely wrong.

WHAT ARE YOUR VULNERABILITIES?

➡ **You don't know where your physical assets are in real time.** Without a dynamic physical inventory of your assets, you are blind in three areas.

> 1. Someone may introduce their own device directly into your network which could cause severe harm to your organisation. For example, an introduction of a foreign laptop, mobile device, a USB, NAS box, etc.
>
> 2. An employee may steal a physical asset without your knowledge.
>
> 3. You have no idea what critical assets need protecting, leaving your organisation unsure of what to address and how to address it.

➡ **You don't know where your sensitive data lives, whether it is overexposed, who is accessing it, and whether it has been changed.** Without such information, you cannot prove to your regulators, management, or your data owners, that your IT controls are stringent and that you provide effective protection around your data.

➡ **You don't know what applications run in your environment in real time.** Without a dynamic inventory of the software applications being used on organisation machines, you risk the situations that an employee may introduce their own software. Under these circumstances, it could be malicious, it could be malware, it could be illegal software, or it could be tools that may cause organisation harm.

➡ **You don't know what vulnerabilities exist on your current network.** Without having the knowledge and visibility of the vulnerabilities that exist within your network on an ongoing basis, you do not know where you are vulnerable and a potential insider can expose your business to potential high level risks.

➡ **You don't monitor in real time what privileged access and rights changes occur to your user accounts.** Without the ability to enforce least privileges onto each account on an on-going basis, you are completely vulnerable for an Insider to commit an Insider fraud, theft, or even sabotage your organisation. You also risk losing compliance and governance over business processes and organisation assets.

➡ **You don't monitor system configuration changes in real time.** Without the ability to detect changes across your entire systems, your security posture is severely weakened. This lack of monitoring provides a signal for a "would be" malicious insider, who likely won't be caught committing an Insider act.

➡ **You don't have the ability to detect abnormal system and related behaviours.** Without the ability to identify abnormal system behaviour (from correlating system and applications logs) in real time, you risk missing threats to your system environment, actionable intelligence, and analytics.

For example: if an Insider is running a Brute Force Attack on your key servers, and you don't notice it, don't know what it would look like, and don't know the characteristics of such an event, you won't know or see that you have an attack you must mitigate.

☛ **You don't have the ability to detect abnormal network behaviours.** Network behaviour anomaly products look at network traffic flow for abnormal behavior, such as malicious traffic hitting your key assets. Without it, you aren't able to spot threats, let alone investigate them.

↳ Case Example : A requisition officer convinced his supervisor that he required privileges to access the entire purchasing system in order to be able to do his work. He then used his privileges to modify the city's database to add a fake vendor, create purchase requisitions and modify the inventory. Over a two-year period, he entered 78 purchase orders for the fake vendor and although no supplies were received, he also authorised payment to the vendor. In total over $250,000 was credited to the vendor bank account, which was owned by his wife.

The case illustrates that with no ability to monitor changes or abnormalities within an organisation, fraud can go undetected for years. This fraud was only detected because a finance clerk noticed irregularities in the paper work accompanying the purchase order.

RECOMMENDATION - WHAT YOU NEED TO DO:

1. **Have a real time view of all your IP assets and devices on your network.** It is a very serious problem when you don't know what is on your network or how any of your systems are configured. The IP asset/device list needs to include the following:

    • Automatic asset discovery;

    • The devices are in your environment (whether it be on your network, web, mobile, cloud or virtual);

    • What is installed on these devices; and

    • The vulnerabilities that exist in your network, and the corresponding threat potential?

2. **Deploy real time Integrity monitoring.** The ability to protect your critical systems will be determined based on whether you are able to detect changes occurring on your critical system. The ability to protect your system will also be based on your ability to understand whether critical items are an avenue for someone to introduce a security risk, a security risk themselves, or an item that can show non-compliance. Real time integrity monitoring needs to include the following:

    • Ability to detect file changes;

    • Ability to detect process changes;

    • Ability to detect configuration changes; and

    • Continuous real time change detection across your entire enterprise environment, including the introduction of unknown foreign devices.

3. **Deploy System Behaviour Anomaly Detection.** The utilisation of System Behaviour Anomaly Detection uses algorithms to 'learn' the normal behaviour, and usage of your ICT systems. In summary, a System Behaviour Anomaly Detection approach includes the following key points.

    • Establish a baseline of normal behaviour - and pinpoint exceptions.

        - Importantly, you want to make sure that you are not being compromised while the baseline takes place.

· Adapt to authorised network changes and usage spikes - yet distinguish the risky anomalies.

· Connect seemingly unrelated events that pose a threat - which are otherwise invisible.

· Monitor the whole enterprise for non-compliant events – continuously and in real time.

· Assess unusual events in the context of their risk to the enterprise.

· Take protective actions to minimize loss instantly – not hours, days, or weeks after the damage is done.

- 6 -
YOU DON'T HAVE REAL TIME USER BEHAVIOUR ANOMALY DETECTION

Insider Threat is about people who expose their organisation to risk.

If we are to manage that risk, we must be able to manage the context. If, for example, we place a child and a knife in the same room, there is perceived level of risk. If we take either knife or child out of the room, there is no risk.

In the following diagram, it is suggested that risk is a combination of assets and people. Most well managed organisations will be able to identify their assets and place appropriate security controls. However, the challenge arises when organisations are unable to, or very poor at, controlling user behaviour. Why? Because they can't. People are free living spirts with their own values, beliefs, thoughts, ideas, likes, dislikes, frustrations, fears and other frameworks that govern their unique behaviour, and those items cannot be placed into a simple controlling box.

According to 2015 Verizon Data Breach Investigation Report, **90% of all security incidents involve people.**

CYBER SECURITY ?

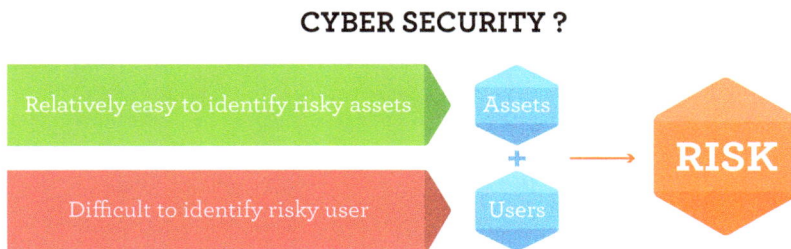

Relatively easy to identify risky assets — Assets

Difficult to identify risky user — Users

Assets + Users → RISK

Having said that, if we place a different context around their environment, their behaviour will change. For example, placing red-light speeding cameras will entice the driver to slow down and not drive through the red light, for fearing of being fined (again, pain vs pleasure).

Why do we place a security camera deep inside a bank's vault? For two reasons: One, so the consumer knows that they are being monitored, and two, so the bank is able to prove who the specific person in the vault is at a specific day and time.

In the digital world, User Behaviour Monitoring solutions directly demonstrate what every user activity generates. Like a virtual camera, User Behaviour Monitoring captures the activities of the user, and provides irrefutable evidence of exactly who did what, when, where, and how.

90%
of all security incidents involve people – Verizon Data Breach Investigation Report

WHAT ARE YOUR VULNERABILITIES?

➡ **You are not able to effectively educate and enforce policies for your employees and other users regarding acceptable behaviour in real time.** At least 50% of all incidents can be prevented by ensuring that employees are aware of online behaviours that can pose risk to the organisation. Although, you may provide regular user awareness security training, you will never be able to enforce corporate policies.

➡ **You are not able to stop or provide deterrence to your employees in real time.** The most effective way to discourage users from performing dangerous or out-of-policy actions is to make sure they understand that all their actions are now being recorded and will be reviewed by the appropriate personnel. Without this ability, you have missed a key part in your strategic approach to create "deterrence" for users acting in a risky way.

➡ **You have no way to detect Insider Incidents to see exactly who did what, when and how.** If an alert is generated, then on-duty personnel can immediately call up a streaming video of the user's session to simultaneously observe what the user is doing, and what they were doing leading up to the security event. Without this ability, you would not be able to identify whether this persons activities are deemed risky or not.

➡ **You have no way to investigate an Insider Incident to see what exactly occurred.** Should an Insider Incident occur, it is important that you possess incontrovertible evidence of exactly what transpired: who did what, when, where and how. Without it, you could spend months collecting sufficient and crucial evidence, which is not only very costly, but time taxing.

➡ **You have no way to identify user behaviour anomalies.** Should an insider behaviour change, it is important to gain immediate insight into the context, and to identify whether the user may pose a risk to the organisation. For example, when an employee leaves their work, their productivity changes prior to resigning. A majority of data theft takes place 30 days before and 30 days after they resign. With no real time visibility of possible user behaviour anomalies, your organisation is very open for a breach.

↳ *Case Example :* After an employee had given notice, he made use of ongoing network access to transfer sensitive internal organisation data to a personal Dropbox instance in order to give himself a head start on his search for a new job. The company was able to analyse his activities which showed them exactly what happened.

The case illustrates that, if a user completes malicious actions, the incident could be concluded in a matter of minutes, not months, if the company is equipped to employ a User Behaviour Monitoring system.

RECOMMENDATION - WHAT YOU NEED TO DO:

Deploy a User Behaviour Monitoring solution on your key assets. When dealing with Insider Threats, the solution must be able to provide you with the following items.

- A complete visibility of employee's activities. Replay user session activities.

- Monitor equally generic user activities as well as privilege users, including the ability to identify who exactly the generic authenticated user is, such as "administrator".

- Visibility of the riskiest users in real time.

- Protect the privacy of your employees. The ability to anonymise data is critically important in order to protect individuals.

- Perform user behaviour profiling for detecting anomaly and inconsistencies. For example, a user that is accessing sensitive data at 3am from a different country should be cause for alarm.

- Threat detection and analysis to investigate and facilitate an investigation.

- The ability to configure behavioural indicators of potential insider threats and automatically detect and trigger suspicious activity.

- The ability to help enforce organisation policies by interacting with users in real time with pop-up messages when their activities breach policies. This also helps educate users about best practices.

- The ability to block users from proceeding when they breach a corporate policy.

- The ability to provide user activity summary for productivity monitoring and general behaviour assessment.

- The ability to integrate with Security Incident Event Management (SIEM) solutions as well as support help desk systems (Information Technology System Management - ITSM).

- 7 -
YOU HAVEN'T INSTITUTED AN INSIDER THREAT PROGRAM

If an organisation wants to establish the appropriate plans to mitigate Insider Threats, it must approach it from a strategic point of view. A tactical approach is a silver bullet solution that partially works, but usually adds to the overall costs without really providing return on investment.

That is why the best approach, usually, is to develop and implement an Insider Threat Program. The key components of an Insider Threat Program are necessary to prepare organisations for handling insider attacks in a consistent, timely, and quality manner.

CERT Insider Threat Centre identified a set of key components that are necessary to produce a fully functioning insider threat program. The full set of components for a successful insider threat program are illustrated in the figure below:

CERT Insider Threat Center Key Components of an Insider Threat Program

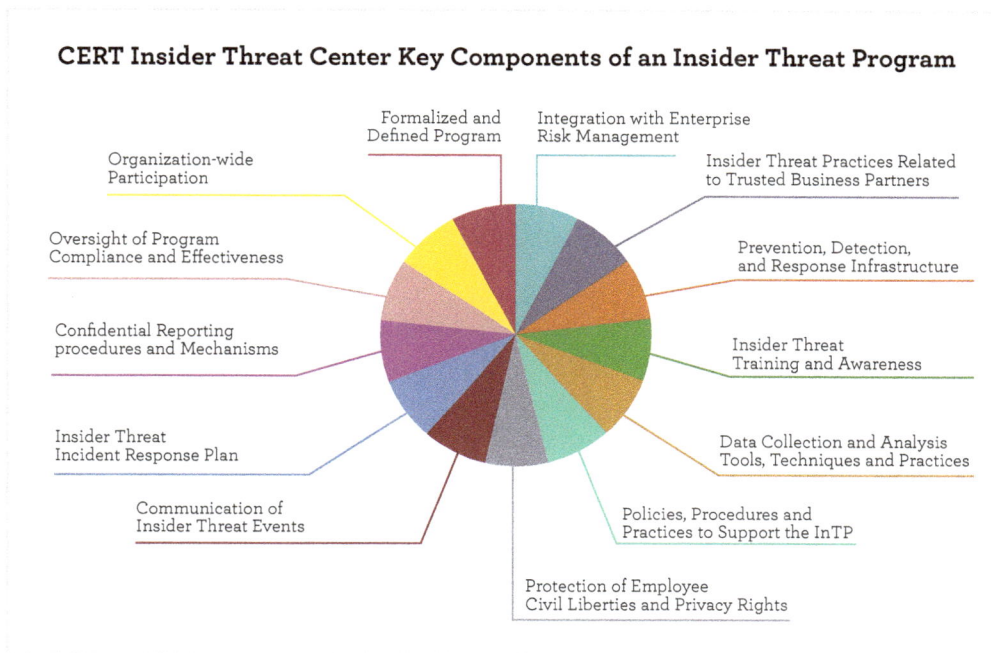

An Insider Threat program is an enterprise-wide program with an established vision and defined roles and responsibilities for those involved.

An Insider Threat Program provides a robust, repeatable set of processes that an organisation can use to prevent or detect suspicious activity and to resolve malicious incidents.

As such, an Insider Threat Program helps organisations detect, prevent and respond to insider incidents. Equally important, it helps in educating and deterring would be potential employees from becoming malicious.

An Insider Threat team is similar to a standard incident response team. Both teams handle incidents, however the Insider Threat team responds to the incidents that are suspected to involve insiders.

Some would argue that they have an established Insider Fraud Team or an Insider Investigation Team. That's all well and good, but the real difference is that an Insider Threat Program is designed to be proactive to mitigate Insider Threats before they happen. An investigator is usually brought in once an incident has occurred (after-the-fact).

WHAT ARE YOUR VULNERABILITIES?

➡ **Failing to have an Insider Threat Program.** Without it, you are not able to handle insider attacks in a consistent, timely, and quality manner.

➡ **There is no support from executives.** Without support and funding from executives, there is no true commitment and focus on mitigating the risk of an Insider Threat.

➡ **There is no collaboration or no communication between different areas of the organisation.** Insider Threats can impact different areas of the organisation, such as Legal, HR, IT, Information Security, Physical Security, and others, so there needs to be cross organization communication/collaboration. Some of the challenges that can arise are:

- Ensuring privacy and confidentiality of the incident;

- Safeguarding evidence;

- Interaction and communication with law enforcement; and

- Identifying the legal ramifications.

↳ *Case Example : An information technology support person had administrator level password access to the organisation network. Late one weekend night, three months after leaving the organisations, the Insider used his administrator account and password to remotely access the organisation network. The Insider changed the passwords of all the organisation IT systems administrators and shut down most of the organisation servers. In addition, he then deleted files from backup tapes that would have enabled the organisation to promptly recover from the intrusion.*

The case highlights the need for an Insider Threat Program. Why?

- There was no clear communication between HR & IT regarding the separation of the technology support person from the organisation.

- The Insider account/s should have been locked or deleted.

- The victim organisation should have had a comprehensive exit procedure.

- The victim organisation should have used a system anomaly detection for ongoing unauthorised changes.

RECOMMENDATION - WHAT YOU NEED TO DO:

Formalise an Insider Threat Program. It sets the tone for the organisation and creates a focal point for awareness about insider threats. A successful insider threat program includes the following items.

• Support and sponsorship from the executives and board.

• Established policies and procedures for addressing Insider Threats that include HR, Legal, Security, and management (enterprise-wide participation).

• Integrated data collection and analysis of both technical and non-technical indicators of potential inside threat activity.

• Established formal process for response, communication and escalation.

• Active insider threat team that meets on a regular basis and maintains a readiness state.

Can it be stopped?

Insider Threat is ever evolving and changing. By building an Insider Threat Program, your organisation can significantly reduce its exposure to the problem and prevent the most damaging insider attacks.

The program must implement the appropriate strategies with the right combination of policies, procedures, technical controls and culture support. Importantly, it requires the cooperation and collaboration of management and executive staff.

What can you do about it?

Unfortunately, it is not practical for every organisation to implement 100% protection against every threat imaginable to every organisation asset.

It is important to focus on protecting your critical information and systems rather than placing significant effort towards protecting relatively unimportant assets.

A realistic and achievable security goal is to protect those assets deemed critical to your mission from both external and internal threats.

Risk is the combination of threat, vulnerability and impact. In this book, we have listed Seven Insider Threat Environments under which your organisation is most certainly under attack. The sooner insider threats are properly acknowledged the better.

Unfortunately, many organisations focus on protecting assets from those external to the organisation and seriously overlook the Insider Threats. Moreover, technology and security solutions designed without consciously acknowledging and accounting for the potential Insider Threats, often leave the role of protection in the hands of some of the potential threats – the Insiders themselves.

A common misconception is that insider threat risk management is the responsibility of IT and information security staff members alone. Unfortunately, that is one of the biggest reasons why insider attacks continue to occur.

A second misconception is that insider threats can be mitigated solely through hardware and software solutions. However, there is no "silver bullet" for stopping insider threats. Remember, you are dealing with people, not machines.

Moving forward, the key question that you need to answer is: How well are you prepared to protect your organisation confidentiality, integrity and availability of your critical assets from Insider Threats? Realise that –

- Insiders may violate the confidentiality of information by stealing it.

- Insiders may affect the integrity of data by modifying it.

- Insiders may/can affect the availability of the organisation assets by sabotaging it.

You need to understand the threat environment under which your organisation operates. The sooner the threat environment can be characterised, the better. For example, a financial institution would be most concerned about internal fraud while a pharmaceutical company will be most concerned about theft of IP.

The purpose of this book is to assist you in correctly identifying your insider threat environment, your vulnerabilities that enable the threat, and potential impacts that could result from insider incidents including financial, operational, and reputational.

The following Checklist Questionnaire will provide you with a simple overview of your resiliency against a potential Insider Threat actor.

If you have answered 'NO' to one or more of these questions, you have an environment within your organisation which most certainly helps Insider Threat Actors 'take advantage' of your organization, and thereby place your organisation at risk.

CHECKLIST QUESTION- NAIRE

Who Are Your Risky Users? Do You Know?

How does this works? Here is a list of questions. Answer the questions with the first answer that comes to your mind.

Well Done! This means that you are confident that you have a working and consistent, reliable and tested process.

Means that you are not certain that your process is working effectively, or if it is executed consistently. This is where you need to focus, and to invest in how you can achieve better resilience against Insider Threats.

	QUESTIONNAIRE	YES	NO
1.	Do you have a proper employee termination process? User accounts are disabled or deleted and all of their organisation equipment has been returned?		
2.	Do your 3rd party contractors follow the same corporate processes and policies as your captive hired employees? Contractors, consultants, partners, vendors, outsourcing organisations?		
3.	Do you pay special attention to those employees that have either resigned or were fired? According to Carnegie Mellon University (CERT – Software Engineering Institute), employees will typically steal data 30 days before they leave.		
4.	Do you carefully and regularly conduct periodic account reviews to avoid privilege creep? Employees should have sufficient access rights to perform their job, but when an employee role change takes place, new privileges may be authorised.		
5.	Do you perform a real time view of account creation and password changes? Lack of real time visibility into account creation, modification, and who authorised the changes can keep you blind to major trouble.		
6.	Do you encourage a culture of "see something", "say something" if staff recognise uncharacteristic behaviour in a colleague? A significant change in a person's behaviour, unexpected or suspicious, may indicate a possible threat.		
7.	Do you incorporate within your Incident Response Plan, the possibility of potential insider threat incidents? An organisation that doesn't keep an account of a potential threat from within, is leaving themselves vulnerable.		
8.	Do you conduct regular risk assessment to identify critical data, business processes and mission critical systems? Assets that have not been identified are more vulnerable to be breached.		
9.	Do you perform or require a comprehensive background check and periodic assessments on prospective employees, contractors, partners and other trusted business partners?		
10.	Do you enforce separation of duties and least privileges? It is critical that a review of positions in the organisation that handle sensitive information or perform critical functions be performed.		

QUESTIONNAIRE		YES	NO
11.	Do you establish a network activity baseline for individual users as well as systems? The question is, how would you know if there has been an anomaly in activity without the ability to differentiate normal from abnormal activity?		
12.	Do you have visibility of where your unstructured data resides and how exposed it is? For example, would you know whether you have any stale data? Or what is deemed as sensitive? Or how much of this data has Global access?		
13.	Do you have real time visibility for the activities and actions your insiders do, including your privilege users? The big question you need to answer is: "who did what?" Without this, you are blind and highly vulnerable to unwanted incidents.		
14.	Do you have an inventory of all your assets that you monitor in real time? Introduction of a new asset, including software or hardware, into your organisation, or an asset leaving your organisation is very risky.		
15.	Can you disable remote access to your organisation systems when an employee or contractor separates from your organisation? There have been countless Insider incident examples of employees able to connect to the organisation months after separation.		
16.	Do you incorporate within your Enterprise Risk Management Plan, the likelihood and impact of insider threat risks? An organisation that doesn't take account of a potential threat from within is leaving themselves vulnerable and unprepared.		
17.	Do you incorporate within your Security Awareness Training Program, the various topics related to insider threats? Your people are the first line of defence. Empowering them by providing insider threat awareness is critical.		
18.	Have you created a best practice approach and policies in how your people can interact with social media sites and still be safe? Social media sites can reveal a great deal about your organisation workings. Attackers often gather information and map your organisation structure and then identify the "right people" to attack.		
19.	Do all employees including management and executives advocate, enforce and comply with all organisation policies? Policies that do not have buy-in from the top, will fail, and will not be enforced equally.		
20.	Do you have a designated resource to address the problem of insider threat? Only by taking appropriate specialised actions, can the organisation effectively detect, prevent, and respond to the unique threats from insiders.		

GLOSSARY

Assets	Organisation assets are separated into four areas – People; Information; Technology; Facilities.
Breach	An incident that results in the confirmed disclosure to an unauthorised party.
Business Partners	Are those people that are either contractors, consultants, vendors, partners or other non-employee people who have been granted authorised access to the organisation networks, systems, and data.
Collusion with Outsiders	Those insiders who are recruited by outsiders, including organised crime, foreign organisations, or Governments, to commit theft, or modify information.
Identity Crime	The misuse of personal or financial identifiers, in order to gain something of value, and / or facilitate other criminal activity.
Incident	A security event that compromises the integrity, confidentiality or availability of an organisation asset.
Insider	According to the Insider Threat division of CERT's definition (www.cert.org/insider-threat), an Insider is defined as a current or former employee, contractor, or business partner who has authorised access to organisation networks, systems, or data.
Insider Fraud	Crimes where an insider perpetrated into, and used, information technology without authorization, to modify, add, or delete organisation data, for personal gain or theft.
Insider Sabotage	Crimes in which an insider uses IT to direct specific harm to an organization, or an individual.
Insider Theft	An insider that uses information technology to steal proprietary information from the organisation, to include industrial espionage.

Insider Threat	According to the Insider Threat division of CERT's definition, a Malicious Insider is someone who has intentionally exceeded, or intentionally used access in a manner that negatively affected the confidentiality, integrity, availability, or physical well-being of the organisation, information or information systems, or workforce.
Insider Threat Privacy	A well rounded Insider Threat Program must consider employee privacy, and at the same time, it must not infringe upon the privacy rights of the individual working for the organisation. Employees need to have clear expectations about what can be performed, and what is expected while at work.
Insider Threat Program	A program that provides a robust, repeatable set of processes that organisations can use to prevent or detect suspicious activity, and to resolve malicious incidents. The program sets the tone for the organisation and creates a focal point for awareness about insider threats.
Insider Threat Type	There is not one "type" of insider threat. Insider Threat Type is a threat to organisation critical assets, based on the motive of the insider and the consequence they impart on the organisation confidentiality, availability, and integrity of the assets.
Trusted Witting Insider	A disgruntled trusted person who, through their actions and nefarious motivation, is placing the organisation at serious harm. For example, someone that provides privilege information to an unauthorised party.
Unintentional Insider Threat	An insider who, through their actions/inactions without malicious intent, causes harm or substantially increases the probability of future serious harm to the confidentiality, integrity, availability of the organisation information, or information systems.
Untrusted Insider	A person that is not authorised to access organisation assets, but has taken advantage of, or compromised a users' credentials, obtaining a backdoor into the system to assume the role of a trusted employee.

Unwitting Insider

An employee who does not know that what they are doing by their actions and behaviour is placing the organisation in serious harm. For example, a person clicking on a malicious email link or placing an unknown USB thumb drive in the company's computers.

ABOUT COMMSNET GROUP

What does CommsNet Group do? CommsNet Group helps companies, Governments and organisations protect the confidentiality, integrity, and availability of critical assets. It does so by helping increase internal security practices in order to mitigate Insider Threats.

What else? CommsNet Group is one of the fastest growing providers of Insider Threat mitigation solutions and services around the world. CommsNet Group is fast becoming the recognised as Australia's leading expert on Insider Threats.

Many of CommsNet Group clients, Governments, insurance companies, financial institutions, telecommunication organisations, and other large enterprise, depend on CommsNet Group to provide a unique and trusted layer of security so that they can manage with greater certainty and clarity in their ability to protect against insider risks.

CommsNet Group solutions have been designed based on Insider Threat Best Practices modules, which enables the client to receive the necessary and needed control and outcome, and achieve their business objectives.

Learn More About CommsNet Group Insider Threats Services?

Checkout out the following strategies to learn more about how to protect your business from Insider Threats

- **Identify** your state of preparedness against Insider Threats

- Place **Prevention** steps against Insider Threats

- Place **Detection** steps to monitor for Insider Threats

- **Respond** to an Insider Threat incident

- Develop Insider Threat **Best Practice** frameworks

For more information, visit our website: **www.commsnet.com.au**

ABOUT
THE
AUTHOR

Back in the old days, when computers were just invented and the Apple II Mac was in high demand, Boaz was teaching basic computing principles in schools. His passion for helping people get the best from information technology started then, and has never stopped.

Today, Boaz has written over 100 information security articles, whitepapers, trust blogs that specifically focus on helping organisation focus on achieving resiliency and best practices.

He has also given numerous security presentations on topics such as: Insider Threats and cyber threats around the world.

Boaz has written two books.

1. **The Essential Guide To Information Technology Security Best Practices**
   (2nd Edition – 2010)

2. **Protecting Your Business From Cyber Attacks In Only 10 Minutes A Day**
   (2015)

Boaz Fischer is also the CEO of CommsNet Group, a company that he founded in 1996 and focuses on helping organisation identify and mitigate Insider Threats.

Boaz is also a passionate self-human developer. Having attained the Master Certification of Neuro Linguistic Programming (NLP) – Understanding the Science Behind the Human behaviour.

www.ingramcontent.com/pod-product-compliance
Lightning Source LLC
Chambersburg PA
CBHW042032220326
41598CB00074BA/7418